The Crocodile

*A Satirical Tale of Absurdity, Society,
and Human Delusion*

A Modern Translation

Adapted for the Contemporary Reader

Fyodor Dostoevsky

Table of Contents

Preface - Message to the Reader

Rebuilding the Greatest Library in Human History

Thousands of years ago, the Library of Alexandria was the heart of global knowledge — a sanctuary where the wisdom of every known civilization was gathered and shared freely.

And then, it was lost.

Now, we're rebuilding it — and you are invited to join us.

At the Library of Alexandria, we've set out to make every book available to *every person on Earth* — not just in print, but in every language, every format, and for every reader.

Here's how we do it:

- **Deluxe Print Editions at True Printing Cost** - Order any book as a high-quality paperback, elegant hardcover, or stunning boxset — and only pay what it costs to print. No markups. No middlemen.
- **Unlimited Access to the Greatest Works** - Enjoy thousands of timeless classics — from Plato to Shakespeare to Tolstoy — in beautiful, modern eBook and audiobook editions. Read and listen without limits — for every reader, everywhere.
- **Modern Translations for Every Language & Dialect** - We're reimagining the classics in clear, accessible language — and translating them into every dialect imaginable. Everyone deserves to understand humanity's greatest ideas.

When you visit **LibraryofAlexandria.com**, you're not just accessing books — you're joining a global movement to restore, preserve, and share the wisdom of civilization.

Join us today at LibraryofAlexandria.com

Together, we'll ensure the light of human wisdom never fades again.

With gratitude,
The Modern Library of Alexandria Team

Visit:

www.libraryofalexandria.com

Or scan the code below:

1

Introduction

Satire and the Stomach:
Absurdity, Ego, and the Grotesque Theater of Society

The Crocodile, first published in 1865, is one of the most unusual and sharply satirical works in Fyodor Dostoevsky's vast literary canon. Subtitled "An Extraordinary Incident," this short story tells the absurd tale of a man who is swallowed whole by a crocodile—yet remains alive and conscious inside the creature's belly. What follows is a masterfully ironic and farcical narrative that explores vanity, intellectual pretension, and the ridiculousness of public discourse, all while mocking bureaucratic absurdities and fashionable ideologies in mid-19th-century Russian society. At first glance, the story seems playful and surreal, a kind of proto-magical-realist fable. But beneath its surface lies a scathing critique of egoism, ideological affectation, and the commodification of human suffering for public spectacle.

Unlike the spiritual tragedies and philosophical epics Dostoevsky is known for—such as Crime and Punishment or The Brothers Karamazov—The

Crocodile embraces the grotesque and ridiculous. It is filled with slapstick scenarios, exaggerated characters, and improbable situations. Yet it is no less serious in its underlying purpose. Through farce, Dostoevsky reveals the absurdities of a society that has lost touch with truth, compassion, and humility. This is not a story about belief—it is a story about pretense. Not about suffering as redemption—but suffering as theater, ego, and delusion.

The plot is as straightforward as it is absurd. Ivan Matveich, a mid-level bureaucrat, visits an exhibition where a live crocodile is on display. Against advice, he taunts the animal and is promptly swallowed. Miraculously, he survives inside the beast and begins speaking from its belly with full lucidity. His wife Elena and his friend and colleague—the story's narrator—stand outside the cage, bewildered. The crocodile's owner refuses to cut it open, citing the animal's high value and the economic injustice of losing such an exotic attraction. Meanwhile, Ivan, far from despairing, begins to view his strange predicament as a unique opportunity: he can now command public attention, offer political commentary from within the crocodile, and finally assert his importance in society.

This surreal premise allows Dostoevsky to unleash a whirlwind of satire. He skewers everything from the vanity of mid-level officials to the soulless logic of capital, from the shallowness of progressive intellectuals to the voyeurism of the urban public. The crocodile becomes a symbol—not just of absurd fate, but of a society that consumes its own humanity in pursuit of spectacle, status, and empty words.

This modern translation of The Crocodile offers a fluid, accessible version of the story that preserves Dostoevsky's biting wit, his comedic pacing, and the layered irony that makes the tale so rich. Though written as a topical response to the Russia of Dostoevsky's time, The Crocodile remains deeply relevant in the age of social media, influencer culture, bureaucratic paralysis, and ideological echo chambers. In a world increasingly shaped by performance and spectacle, the image of a man giving press conferences from inside a crocodile's stomach feels not only plausible—but prophetic.

The Belly of the Beast: Egoism, Spectacle, and the Death of Sincerity

At the heart of The Crocodile lies one of Dostoevsky's favorite targets: the grotesque ego. Ivan Matveich is not a villain, but he is a fool—a man whose hunger for social validation outweighs any desire for genuine experience or self-awareness. His bizarre fate ought to provoke horror, pity, or at least concern. Instead, he sees it as a unique advantage. Now that he is inside a crocodile, people will listen. He will be published, respected, perhaps even revered. The grotesqueness of his situation becomes, in his mind, a kind of credential.

Dostoevsky's satire here is devastating. Ivan's mind doesn't respond to danger or existential threat. It leaps instead to status and discourse. In his surreal captivity, he is no longer worried about escape but about how to use his condition to gain notoriety. He speculates about writing essays from inside the reptile, offering political critiques, perhaps becoming a symbol of the modern era's absurdities. His voice, literally disembodied and echoing from a creature's gut, becomes the perfect image for modern ideological speech: hollow, performative, and cut off from real human experience.

Through Ivan, Dostoevsky critiques not just the individual ego, but the social system that feeds it. Everyone around him is more interested in what the situation means than what it feels like. The crocodile's owner is concerned only with profit. The public flocks to the scene not to rescue Ivan, but to marvel at the spectacle. His wife, far from being grief-stricken, quickly begins entertaining flirtations, hinting at the shallow, self-serving nature of their marriage. Even the narrator—though more grounded—oscillates between amusement and embarrassment, unsure how seriously to take the whole affair.

This is a society in which suffering has become content. The more absurd and grotesque the situation, the more interesting it is to the public. Real pain is invisible; only spectacle matters. In this, Dostoevsky anticipates a modern world of reality television, viral content, and social media fame—where the boundary between genuine experience and performance collapses, and where absurdity is not rejected but rewarded.

Yet Ivan's delusion is not merely social—it is philosophical. He believes he can now speak from a higher perspective. Trapped in an unthinkable situation, he imagines himself as a kind of metaphysical observer, a disembodied intellect unburdened by the messy reality of embodiment. In this, Dostoevsky mocks the kind of idealist or utopian thinker who ignores human suffering in pursuit of abstract truth. Ivan's absurd confidence mirrors the worst traits of both technocratic modernity and radical ideology: detachment from reality, a blind belief in one's own importance, and a disregard for the actual consequences of one's ideas.

In the end, Ivan never escapes the crocodile. Nor does he want to. He becomes a tragicomic image of the ego consumed by its own pretensions—comfortable in absurdity, proud of its own captivity, mistaking the belly of a beast for a throne of truth.

Bureaucracy, Ideology, and
the Enduring Relevance of the Absurd

Dostoevsky did not write The Crocodile in a vacuum. It was originally conceived as a satirical piece aimed at contemporary figures and debates in Russian society. In particular, it mocks the ideological movements of his time—liberalism, utilitarianism, socialism—as they were championed by progressive intellectuals and foreign-influenced theorists. These movements, in Dostoevsky's view, often reduced human beings to abstract principles, treating social change as a matter of mechanical reordering rather than moral transformation.

The crocodile, in this reading, is a symbol of ideological digestion—of how people, once consumed by abstract systems, continue to speak, act, and think, but only from within the belly of something that has already devoured their humanity. Ivan, the man inside the crocodile, becomes a mouthpiece not for truth, but for the absurd rationalizations that arise when ideology replaces experience.

Equally scathing is Dostoevsky's portrayal of bureaucracy. Everyone involved in Ivan's situation turns to paperwork, policies, and procedural logic. The idea of simply freeing him—cutting the crocodile open—is rejected as too costly, too impractical, or too damaging to someone's business interest. The law cannot help him. The economy cannot afford him. The system is paralyzed by its own rules.

Here Dostoevsky paints a society that cannot respond to the obvious, cannot act on compassion, and cannot make room for the irrationality of the human condition. Instead, it debates, deliberates, and rationalizes—while doing nothing. The crocodile becomes a parody of the modern state: an impersonal, inhuman mechanism that swallows people and then refuses to release them.

And yet, for all its absurdity, The Crocodile is also deeply funny. Its tone is light, its pace brisk, its imagery delightfully bizarre. This is Dostoevsky enjoying himself—using humor as a scalpel, not a club. He exaggerates without losing insight. He caricatures without cruelty. And in doing so, he shows that satire, when done well, can reveal deeper truths than tragedy.

For the contemporary reader, The Crocodile offers a disturbingly familiar world. We, too, live in an age of public performance, ideological possession, and bureaucratic inertia. We, too, watch in fascination as the ridiculous becomes reality. We, too, are sometimes tempted to speak from within the belly of spectacle rather than risk the discomfort of honest action.

This translation brings Dostoevsky's wit and warning to life for modern audiences, not merely by updating the words, but by preserving the comedic rhythm, the emotional irony, and the layers of double meaning that make this story such a sharp tool of cultural critique.

Read The Crocodile not as a relic of Russian satire, but as a mirror. A mirror that, like all the best comedy, makes us laugh first—and then makes us think. In Ivan's voice echoing from within the crocodile, we may hear something disturbingly close to our own: the voice that wants to be seen, to be admired, to be taken seriously, even in the most absurd conditions. The voice that, when faced with the ridiculous, does not protest—but adapts.

And in that recognition lies the power of Dostoevsky's most absurd tale—not to amuse us, but to awaken us. To remind us that no matter how ridiculous the world becomes, we still have a choice: to speak truth, to act with compassion, and, when necessary, to cut ourselves free from the belly of the beast.

Chapter 1

On January 13 of this year, 1865, at about half-past twelve in the afternoon, Elena Ivanovna, the wife of my cultured friend Ivan Matveitch, who works in the same department as I do and is also a distant relative, expressed a desire to see the crocodile being exhibited in the Arcade for an admission fee. Since Ivan Matveitch already had his ticket for a trip abroad, not so much for health reasons as to broaden his mind, he was free from official duties that morning and had nothing else to do. He readily agreed to his wife's whim and was, in fact, curious himself.

"Great idea!" he said cheerfully. "Let's go see the crocodile! Before we head to Europe, it's good to get acquainted with its native creatures." With that, he took his wife's arm, and off they went to the Arcade. As their close family friend, I joined them, as I often did. I had never seen Ivan Matveitch in such a lively and agreeable mood before. It's strange how unaware we are of what fate has in store for us.

As we entered the Arcade, Ivan Matveitch was immediately impressed by the grandeur of the building. When we reached the shop where the recently arrived crocodile was on display, he even offered to pay the

11

small admission fee for me—a gesture that had never happened before. Inside the small room, alongside the crocodile, there were cockatoo parrots and a group of monkeys kept in a separate case. Near the entrance, on the left wall, there was a large tin tank resembling a shallow bath. The tank, covered with a thin iron grating, held a few inches of water, and in it lay a massive crocodile. The creature was completely still, looking more like a log than a living animal, seemingly dulled by the damp climate, which clearly didn't suit it. At first, none of us found the crocodile particularly interesting.

"So, this is the crocodile," said Elena Ivanovna with a tone of disappointment. "I thought it would be... something different."

She had likely imagined something more dazzling, perhaps made of jewels. The crocodile's owner, a German man, emerged and looked at us with pride.

"He has every reason to be proud," Ivan Matveitch whispered to me. "He knows he's the only person in Russia exhibiting a crocodile."

This odd remark reflected Ivan Matveitch's unusually cheerful mood, quite different from his usual envious nature.

"I don't think your crocodile is alive," said Elena Ivanovna, irritated by the owner's indifference. Flashing a charming smile to soften her words, she added, "Are you sure it's not stuffed?"

"Oh, no, madam," replied the German in broken Russian. He slid the grate off the tank halfway and poked the crocodile's snout with a stick. The beast stirred faintly, moving its paws and tail slightly, raising its head, and letting out a low snuffle.

"Don't be upset, Karlchen," the German said soothingly, clearly pleased with the attention his pet was getting.

"How horrible that crocodile is! It's really frightening," Elena Ivanovna exclaimed, shuddering dramatically. "I know I'm going to dream about it tonight."

"But it won't bite you in your dreams," the German joked, laughing at his own humor. However, none of us joined in.

"Come on, Semyon Semyonitch," Elena Ivanovna said, turning to me, "let's go look at the monkeys. I love monkeys—they're so adorable! The crocodile is awful."

"Don't worry, my dear!" Ivan Matveitch called out, putting on a show of bravery for his wife. "This lazy relic of the Pharaohs' time won't hurt us." He stayed by the tank, even removing his glove to tickle the crocodile's nose, hoping to make it snort. The German, showing politeness to Elena Ivanovna, followed her to the monkey enclosure.

Everything seemed perfectly normal. Elena Ivanovna was laughing and making jokes about how much the monkeys resembled some of her friends, pointing this out to me and laughing heartily. I couldn't help but laugh too—the resemblance was uncanny. The German wasn't sure whether to laugh or take offense, so he simply frowned. It was then that we heard a terrible, unnatural scream that filled the room. For a moment, I stood frozen, but when I saw Elena Ivanovna screaming as well, I turned around.

What I saw left me paralyzed. Ivan Matveitch was in the crocodile's jaws, caught around the waist. The enormous creature had lifted him off the ground, and Ivan Matveitch was frantically kicking. In one horrifying instant, he was gone—swallowed whole. I stood rooted to the spot, watching the entire process with a strange, detached interest. My only thought in that moment was, "What if it had been me instead of Ivan Matveitch? How unpleasant that would have been!"

The crocodile began by clamping Ivan Matveitch in its jaws and positioning him so it could swallow his legs first. It lifted him up, then pulled him down into its mouth up to his waist. Ivan Matveitch struggled, trying to grab the sides of the tank to escape, but the crocodile kept lifting and swallowing him repeatedly. Little by little, he was disappearing right before our eyes. Finally, with one last gulp, the crocodile swallowed him completely, leaving no trace of him outside its body.

From the crocodile's exterior, we could still see the outline of Ivan Matveitch's form moving inside. I was about to scream when something even more shocking happened. The crocodile, seemingly overwhelmed by the size of its meal, opened its jaws wide once more. With a tremendous hiccup, it briefly allowed Ivan Matveitch's head to pop out, his face filled with despair. For a fleeting moment, his spectacles fell from his nose to the bottom of the tank. It felt as though his face had appeared only to take one last look at the world, to bid farewell to life. But the crocodile made another effort, gave a forceful gulp, and the head vanished—this time for good.

The brief appearance and disappearance of Ivan Matveitch's head was horrifying, but at the same time, there was something absurdly comical about it— perhaps due to its unexpectedness or the falling of the spectacles. I couldn't help myself and burst out laughing. Realizing how inappropriate it was to laugh at such a moment, especially as a close family friend, I quickly composed myself. Turning to Elena Ivanovna with an air of sympathy, I said, "Well, that's the end of poor Ivan Matveitch!"

I can hardly describe how distraught Elena Ivanovna was during the entire ordeal. After her initial scream, she stood frozen, staring at the scene as though in a trance. Her eyes seemed ready to pop out of her head. Then, she let out a piercing wail. I grabbed her hands to calm her. At the same time, the crocodile's owner, who had also been frozen in shock, suddenly clasped his hands and cried out, "Oh, my crocodile! Oh, mein allerliebster Karlchen! Mutter, Mutter, Mutter!"

At his cries, a door at the back of the room flew open, and a rosy-faced, disheveled woman in a cap, clearly the Mutter, rushed in, shrieking and running to the German. Chaos erupted. Elena Ivanovna continued to scream, repeatedly yelling, "Flay him! Flay him!" in a frenzy, as though pleading for someone to skin the crocodile or take revenge.

Meanwhile, the German and his wife were wailing uncontrollably over the crocodile. "He's done for!" the man shouted. "He'll burst any moment; he swallowed an entire government official!"

"Our Karlchen, our dear Karlchen, will die!" sobbed his wife.

"We'll be ruined and left without a livelihood!" the man added.

"Flay him! Flay him! Flay him!" Elena Ivanovna kept shouting, tugging at the German's coat.

"He provoked the crocodile! Why did your man tease my crocodile?" the German shouted back, pulling himself free from her grasp. "If Karlchen bursts, you'll have to pay! Das war mein Sohn, das war mein einziger Sohn!" he cried, as though the crocodile were his only child.

I was deeply annoyed by the selfishness of the German and the cold attitude of his disheveled wife, the Mutter. But what alarmed me even more was Elena Ivanovna's repeated cry of "Flay him! Flay him!" I completely misunderstood her strange outburst. I thought, in her grief over the loss of her beloved Ivan Matveitch, she had momentarily lost her senses and was demanding the crocodile be punished by being skinned. But, as I later discovered, she meant something entirely different.

Embarrassed and glancing uneasily toward the door, I began to beg Elena Ivanovna to calm down and, most importantly, to stop using such a shocking word as "flay." Such a reactionary statement, here in the cultured surroundings of the Arcade—mere steps from the lecture hall where Mr. Lavrov might at that moment be delivering a public address—was both inappropriate and unthinkable. It could easily provoke the scorn of sophisticated society or even inspire ridicule in the satirical cartoons of Mr. Stepanov.

To my horror, my fears were quickly realized. The curtain dividing the crocodile room from the entryway where admission was collected suddenly parted. A man with a mustache and beard appeared in the doorway, leaning far forward but keeping his feet carefully outside the room to avoid paying the entrance fee.

"Such a backward and uncultured demand, madam," the stranger declared, trying to balance precariously while staying outside the room, "shows a lack of proper development. It is a result of insufficient phosphorus in your brain. You will surely be ridiculed in the Chronicle of Progress and mocked in satirical illustrations...."

The man couldn't finish his remarks. The proprietor, realizing in horror that someone was speaking in the crocodile room without paying, rushed at the progressive stranger and punched him. Both vanished behind the curtain for a moment, leaving only muffled sounds of scuffling.

It was then I realized the entire commotion was unnecessary. Elena Ivanovna, as it turned out, was completely innocent. She hadn't been calling for the crocodile to be punished. Instead, she simply wanted the crocodile cut open so her husband could be freed.

"What? You want my crocodile destroyed?" the proprietor yelled, storming back into the room. "No! Let your husband perish before my crocodile does! My father showed crocodiles, my grandfather showed crocodiles, my son will show crocodiles, and I will show crocodiles! Everyone will show crocodiles! I am known throughout Europe, and you are known nowhere! You must pay me a fine!"

"Yes, yes!" added the spiteful German woman. "You will pay since Karlchen is ruined!"

"It's pointless to flay the crocodile," I interjected calmly, eager to take Elena Ivanovna home as soon as possible. "Our dear Ivan Matveitch is probably already in heaven."

"My dear," we suddenly heard a voice say, shocking us all. "My advice is to go straight to the superintendent's office. Without the police, you'll never make this German see reason."

The voice was so unexpected and calm that for a moment we couldn't believe our ears. But we quickly rushed to the crocodile's tank, listening with amazement and disbelief to the muffled words of Ivan Matveitch. His voice was faint, high-pitched, and squeaky, as though it were coming from far away. It sounded like someone trying to shout through a pillow from another room, mimicking distant calls across a plain.

"Ivan Matveitch, my dear, you're alive!" Elena Ivanovna stammered in shock.

Ivan Matveitch's voice came through, faint but steady. "Yes, I'm alive and well," he said, "and thankfully, I've been swallowed without harm. My only worry is how my superiors will view this incident. After all, I got permission to travel abroad and ended up inside a crocodile. It's not exactly clever."

"But, my dear, forget about being clever right now," interrupted Elena Ivanovna. "The first thing we need to do is figure out how to get you out of there."

"Excavate!" the German proprietor cried out. "I won't allow my crocodile to be cut open! Now the public will come in greater numbers, and I will charge fifty kopecks, and Karlchen won't burst anymore."

"Thank God!" his wife added.

"They're right," Ivan Matveitch said calmly. "Economic principles come before anything else."

"My dear, I'm going straight to the authorities to file a complaint. We can't handle this on our own."

"I think that's wise," Ivan Matveitch agreed. "But in these times of economic hardship, cutting open a crocodile without compensation isn't simple. The question is: What will the German take for his crocodile? And how will it be paid? As you know, I don't have the funds."

"Maybe from your salary?" I suggested timidly, but the proprietor immediately cut me off.

"I will not sell the crocodile! For three thousand, maybe I sell! For four thousand, perhaps! Now the public will come even more. I will sell for five thousand!"

His greedy eyes sparkled as he spoke, and his arrogance was insufferable.

"I'm leaving!" I exclaimed, irritated.

"And I will go too! I'll go straight to Andrey Osipitch and beg him," cried Elena Ivanovna.

"Don't do that, my dear," Ivan Matveitch said quickly. He had always been jealous of Andrey Osipitch's refined manners and knew Elena would enjoy pleading with him. "And you," he added, turning to me, "shouldn't rush off in such a reckless way either. Go to Timofey Semyonitch today as if it were just a normal visit. He's old-fashioned and not particularly brilliant, but he's honest and dependable. Send him my regards and explain the situation. Oh, and since I owe him seven roubles from our last card game, pay him back. That will help soften him. His advice might guide us. In the meantime, take Elena Ivanovna home."

"Calm yourself, my dear," he continued, addressing his wife. "All this shouting and fussing has worn me out.

I'd like to rest. It's soft and warm in here, though it's still dark."

"Dark? Then how can you look around?" Elena Ivanovna asked hopefully.

"It's pitch black," Ivan Matveitch replied, "but I can feel my surroundings with my hands. Now, goodbye, and don't worry. Take care of yourself. And you, Semyon Semyonitch, come see me tonight. Tie a knot in your handkerchief to remind yourself."

I was relieved to leave, feeling both tired and bored. Offering my arm to the distraught but still radiant Elena Ivanovna, I hurried her out of the crocodile room.

"The next visit will cost another quarter-rouble," the proprietor called after us.

"They're so greedy!" Elena Ivanovna muttered, glancing at herself in every mirror in the Arcade. She was clearly aware that her distress had only enhanced her beauty.

"It's the principles of economics," I said, proud that passersby could see her on my arm.

"The principles of economics," she repeated, her voice soft and curious. "I didn't really understand what Ivan Matveitch was saying about economics."

"I'll explain," I replied and began recounting an article I had read that morning about the benefits of foreign investment in our country.

"How strange," she interrupted after a while. "But stop, you awful man. What nonsense! Do I look flushed?"

"You look perfect, not flushed at all," I said, using the chance to pay her a compliment.

"Naughty man," she said with a playful smile. Then, after a pause, she added, "Poor Ivan Matveitch. I do feel sorry for him. But how will he eat? And... what if he needs something?"

It was a practical question that hadn't even crossed my mind. Women are often more attentive to such details.

"Poor thing! He's stuck in there with nothing to do, and it's so dark. Oh, how I wish I had a photograph of him! I suppose I'm a kind of widow now," she added with a flirtatious smile. "Hm... I do feel sorry for him."

Her remarks were a natural expression of a young wife's grief, tinged with her usual charm. I finally escorted her home, comforted her, and stayed for dinner. After enjoying a cup of aromatic coffee, I set out for Timofey Semyonitch's house, timing my visit for the evening when most settled families would be at home.

Chapter 2

Timofey Semyonitch greeted me with a hint of nervousness, as though he was slightly uneasy. He led me into his small study and carefully shut the door behind him. "So the children don't disturb us," he explained, clearly a bit flustered. He gestured for me to sit in a chair by his desk, while he settled into an armchair, wrapping the worn edges of his quilted dressing gown around himself. His expression turned serious, almost official, despite the fact that he wasn't my superior or Ivan Matveitch's. Until now, we had regarded him as more of a colleague, even a friend.

"First of all," he began, "let me make it clear that I hold no position of authority here. I'm just another subordinate official, like you and Ivan Matveitch. I have no intention of getting involved in this matter."

I was surprised he seemed to already know what had happened. Nevertheless, I explained the situation in full detail, speaking with genuine concern, as I felt I was fulfilling my duty as a loyal friend. He listened without much surprise but with an air of suspicion.

"You know," he said, "I always thought something like this would happen to him."

"Why, Timofey Semyonitch? This is such an unusual and unexpected event."

"I admit that it's unusual, but his entire career has been leading to this. He was always a bit too reckless, too full of himself—always talking about 'progress' and big ideas. And look where that's gotten him."

"But this is hardly a reflection of progress in general. Surely it's just an unfortunate accident."

"No, it's over-education, I tell you," he said firmly. "Over-education leads people to stick their noses where they don't belong. That's what happened here. But maybe you know better," he added, sounding a bit offended. "I'm just an old man with little education. I started out as a soldier's son, and this year marks my service jubilee."

"Oh no, Timofey Semyonitch, not at all," I replied quickly. "Ivan Matveitch values your guidance greatly. He's eager for your advice, almost pleading for it."

"Pleading for it, is he? Hmph. Crocodile tears, I'd say. I can't believe them. And what was he thinking, planning a trip abroad? He has no money for that sort of thing."

"He saved up from his last bonus," I explained earnestly. "It was only supposed to be a three-month trip—to Switzerland, to see the Alps and maybe visit Naples for spring."

"Naples? Hmph. And for what? Museums? Animals?" Timofey Semyonitch scoffed. "We've got animals here. Bears not far from Petersburg! And now he's become part of a crocodile exhibit himself."

"Please, Timofey Semyonitch, the man is in trouble. He's appealing to you as a friend and elder. Show some compassion—for Elena Ivanovna's sake, at least."

"Ah, his wife?" Timofey Semyonitch's tone softened as he reached for his snuffbox. "A delightful lady. So charming, always tilting her head like that. And such a figure—Andrey Osipitch was praising her just the other day."

"He was praising her?" I asked, a bit startled.

"Yes, and quite enthusiastically. Such eyes, such hair, he said. A real gem, not a lady. And he laughed, of course. He's still young."

"That's a different matter entirely, Timofey Semyonitch."

"Of course, of course. Well then, what do you want me to do?"

Timofey Semyonitch met my request with a measured tone. "Give advice, guidance, as a man of experience, a relative! What are we to do? What steps are we to take? Should we go to the authorities?"

"To the authorities? Absolutely not," Timofey Semyonitch quickly replied. "If you want my advice, the best thing is to keep this quiet and handle it privately. This incident is strange, unheard of, and not at all something to be proud of. Discretion is key here. Let him stay where he is for a while. We need to wait and see."

"But how can we just wait? What if he suffocates in there?"

"Why should he? Didn't you say he seemed relatively comfortable?"

I recounted the entire story again, and Timofey Semyonitch considered it carefully.

"Hm," he murmured, twisting his snuffbox in his hands. "In a way, it's probably good for him to stay there instead of going abroad. Let him reflect on things. Of course, we don't want him to suffocate, so he'll need to take precautions—avoid catching a cough, for example. And as for the German, I believe he's within his rights. After all, it wasn't the German who climbed into Ivan Matveitch's crocodile uninvited. Besides, a crocodile is private property, so we can't simply cut it open without compensation."

"But surely saving a human life matters more than property, Timofey Semyonitch."

"Well, that's a matter for the police. You'll need to involve them."

"But Ivan Matveitch is an important member of the department. What if he's needed?"

"Needed? Ha! Besides, he's on leave. For now, he can 'inspect the countries of Europe' from his current situation. If he doesn't show up when his leave ends, then we'll start asking questions."

"Three months, Timofey Semyonitch! Surely you can see how serious this is?"

"It's his own doing. No one forced him into that crocodile. Are we supposed to assign him a government-paid nurse now? That's not in the regulations. The main issue here is that the crocodile is private property, so the principles of economics apply. And economic principles are essential. Just the other evening, Ignaty Prokofyitch was talking about this at Luka Andreitch's place. Do you know Ignaty Prokofyitch? He's a prominent businessman, very eloquent."

"What was he saying?"

"He was talking about the need for industrial development in our country. According to him, we have too little of it, and to fix that, we need to attract foreign capital. He argued that foreign companies should be encouraged to buy land in Russia, just as they do abroad. Communal landholding, he said, is ruining us. He was passionate about it. He insisted that foreign companies should divide large tracts of land into smaller plots to lease them out. This way, the peasants would have to work harder, knowing they could be evicted. That would supposedly make them more productive and disciplined. In turn, this would bring more money into Russia, create capital, and establish a middle class. He even quoted an article in The Times, which said Russia's finances were weak because we lacked a bourgeoisie, big fortunes, and a compliant working class."

"He certainly sounds convincing," I said.

"He is! He's an orator and plans to present his ideas to the authorities. He even wants to publish them in The News. That's far more substantial than any poetry Ivan Matveitch could write."

Timofey Semyonitch listened as I asked, "But what about Ivan Matveitch?"

He seemed eager to continue his own thoughts, enjoying the chance to show he was well-informed about current issues. "About Ivan Matveitch? I was just getting to that. Here we are, trying to attract foreign capital, and what happens? The moment a foreigner's investment—this crocodile—is doubled in value because of Ivan Matveitch, instead of protecting this capitalist, we're talking about cutting open the source of that capital! Does that make any sense? To me, Ivan Matveitch, as a patriot, should be proud that he's helped double or even triple the crocodile's worth. That's exactly what's needed to bring more capital here. If one crocodile does well, another foreigner might bring one, and then another might bring several. Capital will grow around them—that's how you create a middle class. It must be encouraged."

"Timofey Semyonitch," I exclaimed, "you're asking for an almost superhuman level of sacrifice from poor Ivan Matveitch!"

"I'm asking nothing," he replied firmly. "And let me remind you, I'm not in a position of authority, so I can't demand anything. I'm speaking as a patriot, not as a government official. But let's be honest—why did he get into the crocodile in the first place? A respectable man, married, and in government service—then he does something like this! Is that consistent behavior?"

"But it was an accident!" I protested.

"Who can say? And where will we get the money to compensate the owner?"

"Maybe from his salary?" I suggested hesitantly.

"Would that be enough?"

"No, it wouldn't," I admitted sadly. "At first, the owner was worried the crocodile might burst, but as soon as he realized it was fine, he became delighted at the idea of charging more for entry."

"Not just double, but maybe triple or quadruple!" Timofey Semyonitch chuckled. "The public will rush to see it now, and crocodile owners are clever businessmen. Besides, it's not Lent yet, so people are looking for entertainment. That's why I say Ivan Matveitch should keep a low profile. Everyone might hear he's inside the crocodile, but it doesn't need to be officially confirmed. For now, people think he's abroad. If rumors start, we'll deny them. The important thing is patience—why rush?"

"But what if something happens to him?"

"Don't worry; he's healthy."

"And afterward, when he's waited?"

"Well," Timofey Semyonitch admitted, "this is an unprecedented situation. There's no guide for handling something like this. It will take time."

A sudden idea struck me. "Couldn't he petition to remain officially employed while inside the crocodile? He could be considered on special assignment."

"Without pay, perhaps."

"But why not with pay?" I argued.

"On what grounds?"

"As part of a special commission—to study the crocodile from the inside. It could be a scientific exploration. Observing digestion or habits—gathering data on the spot."

Timofey Semyonitch thought about it. "Sending someone inside a crocodile for research? It's absurd and not in the regulations. And what exactly would he report?"

"He could study nature—like digestion or behavior. It would advance knowledge."

"But would lying inside a crocodile allow someone to do their duties properly? That would be a novelty and a risky one. Again, there's no precedent."

"Well," I said, "no one's ever brought a live crocodile here before."

"Hmm… yes," he said, thinking again. "Your point is valid, and it might justify taking further action. But consider this: if living crocodiles become commonplace and government clerks start disappearing into them, claiming they're comfortable there, and then expect official approval for staying inside, it would set a bad example. Everyone would want to follow suit and get paid for doing nothing."

"Please, do what you can for him, Timofey Semyonitch. By the way, Ivan Matveitch asked me to give you seven roubles he lost to you at cards."

"Ah, yes, he lost that the other day at Nikifor Nikiforitch's. I remember. He was so cheerful and full of life then—and now!" The old man's voice softened with genuine emotion.

"Help him, Timofey Semyonitch!"

"I'll do my best. I'll inquire informally, as though I'm just gathering information. In the meantime, why don't you find out discreetly how much the owner might accept to part with his crocodile?"

Timofey Semyonitch's tone became noticeably warmer.

"Certainly," I replied. "I'll let you know as soon as I find out."

"And his wife... is she managing? Is she very upset?"

"You should visit her, Timofey Semyonitch."

"I've been thinking of it; this would be a good opportunity. But what on earth made him want to see that crocodile? Though, to be honest, I'd like to see it myself."

"You should visit the poor man, Timofey Semyonitch."

"I will, though I don't want to give him false hope. I'll go as a private individual... Well, good-bye. I'm off to Nikifor Nikiforitch's again. Will you be there?"

"No, I'm going to check on the poor prisoner."

"Yes, now he's truly a prisoner! Ah, this is what comes of being careless."

I said goodbye to the old man. My thoughts wandered as I left. Timofey Semyonitch was a kind and honorable man, yet as I walked away, I found myself reflecting on how rare people like him had become, especially after fifty years of service.

Without delay, I headed to the Arcade to share the news with poor Ivan Matveitch. I was also driven by curiosity to see how he was managing inside the crocodile. Could someone really live inside a crocodile? Was it even possible? At times, the whole situation seemed so bizarre and unreal, like a surreal nightmare— especially since the central figure in it all was such an absurd and monstrous creature.

Chapter 3

And yet, this wasn't a dream but an undeniable reality. Would I be telling this story if it weren't true? Let me continue.

It was late, around nine in the evening, when I reached the Arcade. I had to enter the crocodile room through the back door because the German owner had closed the shop earlier than usual. In the privacy of his home, he was wandering around in an old, greasy frock-coat, looking three times happier than he had that morning. Clearly, he wasn't worried anymore, as more people had been visiting the exhibit. A little later, his wife, the Mutter, came out, likely to keep an eye on me. The German and the Mutter whispered to each other often. Even though the shop was closed, he still charged me a quarter-rouble. Such unnecessary precision!

"You will pay every time. The public pays one rouble, but you only pay a quarter because you are a good friend of your good friend. And I respect friends," he explained.

"Are you alive? Are you alive, my cultured friend?" I called out as I approached the crocodile, hoping my voice would flatter Ivan Matveitch.

"Alive and well," he replied, sounding distant, as though speaking from under a bed, even though I was right next to him. "Alive and well. But we'll discuss that later. How are things going?"

Ignoring his question, I quickly began asking how he was, what it was like inside the crocodile, and what he could see. Both friendship and basic courtesy demanded it. But, as usual, he cut me off with an impatient tone.

"How are things going?" he snapped, his voice high-pitched and, at that moment, particularly grating.

I reluctantly described my entire conversation with Timofey Semyonitch in great detail, making sure my irritation was clear in my tone.

"The old man is right," Ivan Matveitch declared abruptly, as he often did. "I respect practical people and can't stand sentimental fools. That said, your idea about a special commission isn't entirely stupid. I do have a lot to report—both scientifically and ethically. But now, everything has changed unexpectedly, and worrying about a salary seems trivial. Listen carefully. Are you sitting down?"

"No, I'm standing," I replied.

"Sit on the floor if you have to, but listen closely," he ordered.

Annoyed, I grabbed a chair and slammed it down onto the floor before sitting.

"Listen," he began in his usual authoritative tone. "The public came in droves today. By evening, there was no space left, and the police had to come to maintain order. At eight, the owner decided to close early to count the day's earnings and prepare for tomorrow. I already know tomorrow will be like a carnival. All the most cultured people of the capital, ladies of high society, foreign ambassadors, leading lawyers, and others will come. People from the farthest corners of our vast empire will flock here. The bottom line is, I am now the center of attention. Though out of sight, I am at the forefront. I'll teach the idle masses and serve as an example of dignity and acceptance. I will become a kind of teacher for humanity. Even the biological observations I can provide from inside this creature are invaluable. So, rather than despairing, I am confidently looking forward to a brilliant career."

"You won't find it dull?" I asked sarcastically.

Here's the revised text:

What annoyed me most was the overblown way he spoke. Still, it left me unsettled. "What could this shallow fool possibly be so full of himself about?" I muttered. "He should be crying, not acting all high and mighty."

"No!" he shot back sharply. "I'm full of great ideas. Only now can I finally reflect on how to improve humanity's condition. Truth and enlightenment will emerge from this crocodile. I'll develop a brand-new economic theory and take pride in it—something I couldn't do before because of my job and other petty distractions. I'll refute everything and become a new Fourier. By the way, did you give Timofey Semyonitch the seven roubles?"

"Yes, out of my own pocket," I replied, trying to emphasize that fact.

"We'll settle that," he said arrogantly. "I'm sure my salary will be raised. Who deserves it more than me? I'm more valuable than ever now. But let's move on. My wife?"

"You mean Elena Ivanovna?" I asked cautiously.

"My wife?" he practically screeched.

I had no choice. Grinding my teeth, I told him how I had left Elena Ivanovna. He didn't even let me finish.

"I have special plans for her," he began impatiently. "If I'm going to be famous here, I want her to be celebrated out there. Scholars, poets, philosophers, foreign scientists, and politicians will talk with me in the morning, then visit her salon in the evening. Starting next week, she must host an 'At Home' gathering every night. With my doubled salary, we can afford to entertain. Just tea and a few hired servants—simple. People will talk about both of us. I've wanted fame for so long but couldn't achieve it because of my modest position. Now, one gulp from a crocodile has changed everything. Every word I say will be noted, repeated, and published. I'll show them what they've been missing! 'This man could have been a foreign minister or ruled a nation,' they'll say. And some will argue, 'Yet he didn't rule a nation.' How am I less deserving than those other leaders? My wife will match my greatness—brains on my part, beauty on hers. Some will say, 'She's beautiful because she's his wife,' while others will argue, 'She's his wife because she's beautiful.' To prepare, Elena Ivanovna should buy Kraevsky's Encyclopaedia tomorrow so she can discuss any topic. She must also read the political editorials in the Petersburg News and compare them daily with the Voice. I imagine the crocodile's owner might even agree to let me attend her salon inside a tank. I'll dazzle the guests with witty remarks prepared in advance. I'll share plans with the politicians, speak poetry to the poets, and charm the ladies without making their husbands jealous—after all, I'm no threat. I'll also serve as a symbol of dignity and acceptance. Elena Ivanovna will become a celebrated literary figure. She'll embody the finest virtues, and if they call Andrey Alexandrovitch the Russian Alfred de Musset, they'll call her the Russian Yevgenia Tour."

I couldn't help but wonder if he was feverish or delirious. It was the same Ivan Matveitch, but now exaggerated beyond belief.

"My friend," I asked, "are you planning to live long in there? Tell me honestly, how do you eat, sleep, or breathe? I'm asking as a friend, and you must admit this situation is unnatural. My curiosity is only natural."

"Idle curiosity, nothing more," he declared pompously. "But I'll humor you. You want to know how I manage inside this monster? First, to my amusement, I've discovered the crocodile is completely empty inside. It's like a huge, hollow sack made of gutta-percha, similar to those stretchy goods sold in Gorokhovaya Street or Morskaya. Otherwise, how could there possibly be room for me?"

"Is it really possible?" I exclaimed, completely astonished. "Can the crocodile truly be hollow inside?"

"Absolutely," Ivan Matveitch insisted with a stern and authoritative tone. "And most likely, this is exactly how nature intended it. A crocodile has nothing but jaws filled with sharp teeth and a long tail—those are its defining features. The middle part, between its jaws and tail, is simply an empty space surrounded by something like gutta-percha. It's probably made from gutta-percha itself."

"But what about the ribs, the stomach, the intestines, the liver, the heart?" I interrupted angrily.

"There's none of that—absolutely nothing. And I doubt there ever was. Those are just fanciful tales from unreliable travelers. Right now, I'm essentially inflating the crocodile from the inside with my body, much like how one fills an air cushion. The creature is surprisingly elastic. In fact, as a close family friend, you could even join me inside if you had the courage and generosity— and there would still be space left over. I'm even considering inviting Elena Ivanovna to join me in the future. But this hollow, empty structure of the crocodile aligns perfectly with the principles of natural science.

Think about it: if someone were to design a crocodile from scratch, they would first need to identify its primary function. The obvious answer is to swallow people. And how can one ensure that the crocodile can swallow humans? The answer is clear—it must be hollow inside. Physics tells us that nature abhors a vacuum. So, the crocodile must have an empty interior, driving it to fill that space with whatever it encounters. This explains why crocodiles swallow humans.

Of course, the same logic doesn't apply to humans. For example, the emptier a person's head is, the less they seem to feel the need to fill it—one notable exception to the general rule. All of this has become perfectly clear to me now. Being inside this creature, I feel as though I'm in the very heart of nature itself, studying its secrets firsthand. Even the word 'crocodile' supports my theory. It originates from 'crocodillo,' an Italian term that likely dates back to the era of the Egyptian pharaohs. The root of the word is connected to the French verb 'croquer,' which means to eat, devour, or absorb. This will form the basis of my first lecture in Elena Ivanovna's salon when I make my appearance in a tank."

"My friend, shouldn't you consider taking some kind of purgative?" I blurted out, unable to hold back my concern.

"Fever—he's feverish," I muttered to myself anxiously.

"Don't be ridiculous," he replied, full of contempt. "Besides, taking medicine would be terribly inconvenient in my current situation. I knew you'd suggest something like that."

"But how are you managing to eat?" I asked. "Have you had anything to eat today?"

"No, but I'm not hungry. In fact, I suspect I may never need to eat again. It's entirely logical. By occupying the crocodile's interior, I'm making it feel perpetually full. Now it won't need feeding for years. At the same time, as I nourish the crocodile, it nourishes me by sharing its vital juices. It's similar to how some coquettes preserve their beauty by sleeping wrapped in raw steak. After a morning bath, they emerge looking fresh and radiant. This mutual nourishment benefits both of us.

Of course, digestion won't be easy for the crocodile—it isn't built to process someone like me. That's why I try not to move too much, even though I could. I don't want to cause unnecessary discomfort to the poor creature. This is one small drawback of my situation. Timofey Semyonitch was right in a way when he said I was lying there like a log. But I'll prove that even lying like a log can inspire revolutionary ideas for humanity. In fact, most of the groundbreaking ideas and movements we see in newspapers and magazines come from people who are, metaphorically speaking, lying like logs. Critics may call them disconnected from reality, but what does that matter?

Right now, I'm developing my own complete system. You wouldn't believe how easy it is! Just retreat into a quiet corner—or in my case, a crocodile—close your eyes, and you can dream up a perfect future for humanity. Since you left this afternoon, I've already devised three different systems, and I'm working on a fourth. True, you have to first dismantle everything that came before, but that's much easier to do from within the crocodile.

There are only minor inconveniences in my position. It's slightly damp, there's a slimy coating, and it smells faintly of rubber—like my old galoshes. But beyond that, there's nothing to complain about."

"Ivan Matveitch," I interrupted, "this all sounds unbelievable! And are you seriously planning never to eat again?"

"Why are you so focused on trivial nonsense, you shallow creature?" he snapped. "Here I am, discussing grand ideas, and you're worried about dining! Understand this—I am sustained by the great ideas illuminating the darkness surrounding me. That said, the kind-hearted proprietor, after consulting with his thoughtful Mutter, has decided to insert a bent metal tube, like a whistle, into the crocodile's jaws each morning. Through it, I can sip coffee or broth with soaked bread. The tube is already being crafted nearby. But honestly, this seems like an unnecessary luxury to me.

I expect to live for at least a thousand years if crocodiles really do live that long. By the way, you should verify this in a natural history book tomorrow and let me know—I might be confusing them with some prehistoric creature. One concern troubles me, though: since I'm wearing clothes and boots, the crocodile obviously cannot digest me. Moreover, I'm alive, so my willpower actively resists digestion. You can understand why I'd rather not become what all food eventually turns into—it would be far too degrading.

However, I do fear that over a thousand years, my clothing, unfortunately made of Russian fabric, might disintegrate. Without it, I could risk digestion against my will, perhaps while I sleep, when one has no control. The idea of such humiliation enrages me! This alone supports revising tariffs and encouraging the import of stronger English fabrics, which could withstand nature longer when one is swallowed by a crocodile. I will share this thought with a statesman or a political writer in Petersburg's newspapers. They should spread the idea widely. This won't be the only concept they'll take from me. I predict that every morning, reporters armed with quarter-roubles from their editors will flock here to gather my thoughts on the latest telegrams. The future, my friend, looks exceptionally bright!"

"Fever—he's delirious," I muttered under my breath.

"My friend, what about freedom?" I asked, trying to understand his views. "You're essentially in prison, and isn't freedom a basic right?"

"You're a fool," he replied. "Savages crave independence; wise men value order. And if there's no order—"

"Ivan Matveitch, I beg you, stop!" I pleaded.

"Silence and listen!" he barked, irritated by my interruption. "My spirit has never soared higher than it does now. In my small refuge, my only concern is the critique I might face from literary magazines or the satire in our newspapers. I dread that ignorant visitors, jealous people, or nihilists might ridicule me. But I'm taking precautions. I eagerly await the public's reaction tomorrow, particularly from the newspapers. You must bring me updates from them."

"All right. I'll bring a stack of papers tomorrow," I promised.

"Tomorrow's too early for the articles; it'll take four days for the news to spread. But starting today, visit me each evening through the back way. I'll need you as my secretary. You'll read newspapers and magazines aloud while I dictate my ideas and assign tasks. Don't forget the foreign telegrams—make sure I get all the European updates daily. But enough of this; you're probably tired. Go home, and don't dwell on my earlier worries about criticism. I'm not truly afraid of it. Critics are in a precarious position themselves. One must simply be wise and virtuous to rise above. Whether as Socrates,

Diogenes, or perhaps both combined—that's my destined role for humanity."

Ivan Matveitch spoke with such arrogance and feverish excitement, like someone too restless to keep a secret. Everything he claimed about the crocodile struck me as dubious. Could it truly be hollow inside? I suspected he was boasting out of vanity or to demean me. True, he was unwell, and allowances had to be made, but I must confess I had never been fond of Ivan Matveitch. For years, I had tried to escape his influence, but I always found myself drawn back, as though hoping to prove something or to take revenge. Friendship can be such a peculiar thing! Honestly, nine-tenths of my connection to him stemmed from malice. Still, on this occasion, we parted with a genuine sense of camaraderie.

"Your friend is a very clever man," the German muttered as he escorted me out. He had been listening closely to our conversation.

"By the way," I said, seizing the opportunity, "how much would you sell your crocodile for, in case someone wanted to buy it?"

Ivan Matveitch, who overheard the question, waited eagerly for the response. It was clear he didn't want the German to undervalue the creature; he even cleared his throat in a peculiar way.

At first, the German reacted with outrage. "No one will dare to buy my crocodile!" he shouted, turning as red as a boiled lobster. "I won't sell him! Not for a million thalers! Today, I made one hundred and thirty thalers, and tomorrow I'll make ten thousand, then a hundred thousand every day! I will not sell him!"

Ivan Matveitch chuckled with satisfaction. Struggling to remain calm—for I felt it was my duty as his friend—I calmly pointed out to the delusional German that his calculations might be flawed. If he truly made one hundred thousand roubles a day, then in just four days, all of Petersburg would have visited, leaving no one else to bring him money. I added that life and death are in God's hands, the crocodile might burst, or Ivan Matveitch could fall ill and die.

The German looked thoughtful.

"I will get him drops from the chemist to make sure your friend does not die," he said after some consideration.

"Drops might help," I replied, "but consider that this could become a legal matter. Ivan Matveitch's wife may demand her husband's release. You're hoping to get rich from this, but do you plan to provide Elena Ivanovna with a pension?"

"No, I do not intend to," the German said firmly.

"No, we do not intend to," the Mutter echoed, her tone even harsher.

"Then wouldn't it be better to accept a guaranteed sum now? Something moderate but secure, rather than leaving it all to chance? Of course, I'm only asking out of curiosity."

The German pulled the Mutter aside, and they whispered together in a corner near a case holding the largest and ugliest monkey in their collection.

"You'll see," Ivan Matveitch said confidently.

At that moment, I was overwhelmed by the desire to give the German a beating, then to give the Mutter an even worse one, and finally to deliver the hardest thrashing of all to Ivan Matveitch for his absurd vanity. But all of that paled in comparison to the ridiculous demand the greedy German made after consulting the Mutter.

He asked for fifty thousand roubles in government bonds with lottery vouchers, a brick house on Gorohovy Street with a chemist's shop attached, and, as if that weren't absurd enough, the rank of a Russian colonel.

"You see!" Ivan Matveitch exclaimed triumphantly. "I told you so! Apart from his silly desire to be made a colonel, he fully understands the economic value of this situation. The economic principle comes first!"

"Are you serious?" I shouted at the German, furious. "Why should you be made a colonel? What heroic deed have you performed? What service have you rendered? You're insane!"

"Insane?" the German shouted back, offended. "No, I am very sensible, but you are very stupid! I deserve to be a colonel because I show a crocodile with a live hofrath inside! A Russian cannot show a crocodile with a live hofrath inside! I am extremely clever and deserve to be a colonel!"

"Goodbye, Ivan Matveitch!" I yelled, trembling with anger, and stormed out of the crocodile room.

I could feel myself losing control and knew I couldn't take another minute of their absurdity. The cold night air cooled my temper slightly. After spitting on the ground several times in frustration, I hailed a cab and went home. Once there, I undressed, threw myself into bed, and fumed.

What angered me the most was that I had somehow ended up as his secretary. Now I would be stuck there every evening, bored out of my mind, all in the name of friendship. I wanted to kick myself for agreeing to it, and I did—after blowing out the candle and pulling the blankets over my head, I punched myself several times out of frustration. It helped a little, and eventually, I fell into a deep sleep, exhausted.

All night, I dreamed of nothing but monkeys. By morning, though, my dreams shifted to Elena Ivanovna.

Chapter 4

The monkeys appeared in my dreams, no doubt because they were locked up in the German's display case. But dreaming of Elena Ivanovna was an entirely different matter.

I should admit right away that I loved her, but I must clarify this immediately: I loved her like a father loves a child, nothing more. I know this because I often felt an irresistible urge to kiss her little head or her rosy cheek. Though I never acted on these feelings, I wouldn't have objected to kissing her lips either—or even her teeth, which gleamed so beautifully like rows of tiny pearls whenever she laughed. And she laughed a lot. Ivan Matveitch, during his more affectionate moments, used to call her his "darling absurdity," which was a perfectly fitting name. She was a delightful little creature, like a sweet confection—simple as that. That's why I've never understood how Ivan Matveitch could have imagined his wife as some kind of Russian intellectual heroine.

Anyway, aside from the monkeys, my dream left me with a pleasant feeling. While sipping my morning tea and reflecting on everything that had happened the day before, I decided to visit Elena Ivanovna before heading to the office. As their family friend, it was the natural thing to do.

In a small room adjacent to the bedroom, which they grandly called the "little drawing room" (though their larger drawing room wasn't much bigger), Elena Ivanovna sat in a light, sheer morning robe. She was lounging on a dainty little sofa in front of a small tea table, sipping coffee from a tiny cup and dipping a delicate biscuit into it. She looked stunningly beautiful but also seemed a bit preoccupied.

"Ah, it's you, you naughty man!" she greeted me with a distracted smile. "Sit down, you featherbrain. Have some coffee. What were you up to yesterday? Were you at the masquerade?"

"Me? No, I don't go to those things," I replied. "Besides, I spent yesterday visiting our captive..." I sighed and adopted a solemn expression as I took a sip of coffee.

"Who?... What captive?... Oh, yes! Poor thing! How is he? Is he bored? You know..." She paused briefly, as if considering her words. "I wanted to ask you something... Do you think I can get a divorce now?"

"A divorce?" I exclaimed, nearly spilling my coffee in shock. My thoughts immediately turned bitterly to the swarthy fellow—a certain dark-skinned man with a small mustache who often visited them and had a knack for amusing Elena Ivanovna. I must confess, I despised him. There was no doubt in my mind that he had seen Elena Ivanovna the day before, either at the masquerade or perhaps even here, and had filled her head with nonsense.

"Well," she rattled off quickly, as though reciting a rehearsed speech, "if he's planning to stay inside that crocodile, maybe forever, while I sit here waiting for him! A husband is supposed to live at home, not inside a crocodile…"

"But this was an unforeseen accident," I began, clearly agitated.

"Oh, don't start," she interrupted, suddenly sounding annoyed. "You're always against me, you villain! I can never get any advice from you! Other people tell me I can get a divorce because Ivan Matveitch won't be getting his salary anymore."

"Elena Ivanovna! Is this really you speaking?" I exclaimed, full of righteous indignation. "Who could have planted such a wicked idea in your mind? Divorce, over something as trivial as a salary, is simply unthinkable. And poor Ivan Matveitch is burning with love for you, even from inside the belly of the beast. Why, he's melting with love—like a lump of sugar. Just yesterday, while you were off enjoying the masquerade, he said that as a last resort, he might send for you, his lawful wife, to join him in the crocodile. Apparently, it's spacious enough inside to fit two—maybe even three—people."

I proceeded to relay the most interesting parts of my conversation with Ivan Matveitch from the night before.

"What, what!" she exclaimed, visibly surprised. "You expect me to crawl inside the crocodile too? With Ivan Matveitch? What a ridiculous idea! How on earth would I even get in there—in my hat and crinoline? Good heavens, how absurd! And what would I look like climbing into it? What if someone saw me? It's ridiculous! And what would I eat in there? And... and... what would I even do there? Oh, this is so absurd! And what if there's a smell of gutta-percha? What if Ivan Matveitch and I had a fight—would we still have to sit there together? Ugh, how awful!"

"I agree, I absolutely agree with all of your points, dear Elena Ivanovna," I interrupted, trying to speak with the natural enthusiasm that comes when you know the truth is on your side. "But there's one thing you've overlooked: he cannot live without you. By inviting you to join him, he's proving his love—passionate, faithful, and devoted love. You've underestimated his feelings for you, my dear Elena Ivanovna!"

"I won't listen! I won't, I won't!" she cried, waving me off with her delicate hand, her freshly washed and polished pink nails catching the light. "You horrid man! You'll make me cry! If you like the idea so much, go get in there yourself. You're his friend, aren't you? Join him, and you can spend the rest of your lives discussing some boring science together."

"You shouldn't mock this suggestion," I said with dignity, trying to rein in her frivolous attitude. "Ivan Matveitch has already invited me. You, of course, are called by duty as his wife. For me, it would be an act of generosity. But last night, when Ivan Matveitch described the elasticity of the crocodile, he hinted that there would be room for not just you two, but even for me as the family friend, should I choose to join."

"What? All three of us?" she exclaimed in astonishment, looking at me. "How could we all possibly fit in there together? Ha-ha-ha! You two are ridiculous! Ha-ha-ha! I'll be pinching you both the whole time, you wretch! Ha-ha-ha! Ha-ha-ha!"

She collapsed onto the sofa, laughing so hard that tears filled her eyes. Her laughter and tears were so enchanting that I couldn't resist rushing to kiss her hand. She didn't pull it away, though she did pinch my ear lightly in playful reconciliation.

We soon grew cheerful, and I explained Ivan Matveitch's plans in detail. The thought of her evening gatherings and her salon seemed to delight her.

"But I'd need so many new dresses," she said thoughtfully. "Ivan Matveitch will have to send me as much of his salary as he can, as soon as he can. Only... only I'm not sure about one thing," she added, pausing. "How will he be brought here in the tank? That's just absurd. I don't want my husband paraded around in a tank. It would be so embarrassing for my guests to see that... I simply can't allow it."

"By the way," she asked suddenly, "was Timofey Semyonitch here yesterday?"

"Oh yes, he was," she replied. "He came to comfort me, and do you know, we played cards the entire time. He played for sweets, and if I lost, he insisted on kissing my hands. What a scoundrel! Can you believe he almost went to the masquerade with me?"

"He was overcome by your charm!" I remarked. "And who wouldn't be, you enchantress?"

"Oh, stop with your flattery! Here, let me give you a pinch as a parting gift. I've gotten quite good at pinching lately. What do you think of that? By the way, did Ivan Matveitch talk about me much yesterday?"

"Well... not exactly," I admitted hesitantly. "He's more focused on the fate of humanity now. He wants—"

"Oh, stop right there!" she interrupted. "I don't want to hear it. It sounds terribly boring. I'll go visit him someday—tomorrow, perhaps. But not today; I have a headache, and besides, there'll be so many people there. They'll point at me and say, 'That's his wife,' and I'll feel so embarrassed. Goodbye. You'll be there this evening, won't you?"

"Yes, to see him. He asked me to bring him the papers."

"That's perfect. Go read to him. But don't come see me today. I'm not feeling well, and I might go visit someone. Goodbye, you naughty man."

"It's that swarthy fellow visiting her tonight," I thought bitterly.

At work, I made sure to show no signs of the worries and troubles weighing on me. However, I soon noticed that some of the most progressive newspapers were being passed around the office unusually quickly, and my colleagues were reading them with unusually serious expressions. The first one that made its way to me was the News-sheet, a paper with no strong political leanings but a general humanitarian focus, which meant it was often looked down on by my colleagues, though they still read it. To my surprise, I found the following paragraph:

"Yesterday, peculiar rumors spread through the broad streets and grand buildings of our vast city. A certain well-known gentleman of high society, perhaps tired of the food at Borel's and the X. Club, visited the Arcade, where a massive crocodile recently brought to the city is being exhibited. The man reportedly arranged with the owner to prepare the crocodile for his dinner. After striking a deal, he began carving pieces off the living creature with a penknife and eating them at an extraordinary speed. Bit by bit, the entire crocodile disappeared into the depths of his stomach. He was even said to have been eyeing an ichneumon, a small animal often kept with crocodiles, perhaps thinking it would taste just as good.

"We have no objection to this new culinary trend, which has long been popular among foreign food enthusiasts. In fact, we predicted its arrival. English lords and adventurers in Egypt organize trips to catch crocodiles and enjoy their meat, cooked like steak with mustard, onions, and potatoes. The French, who followed Lesseps, prefer baking the crocodile's paws in hot ashes—a practice mocked by the English. Both methods would likely gain fans here. We welcome this new industry, which our diverse and resource-rich country desperately needs. Within a year, hundreds of crocodiles could be brought here to replace this one, now lost in the belly of a Petersburg gourmet.

"Why not breed crocodiles in Russia? If the Neva River is too cold for these fascinating creatures, there are ponds in the city and rivers and lakes outside it. Why not raise crocodiles at Pargolovo, Pavlovsk, the Presnensky Ponds, or Samoteka in Moscow? They could provide a unique and nutritious option for refined diners, entertain ladies strolling by the water, and teach children about natural history. Crocodile skin could be used for making jewelry boxes, wallets, cigar cases, and other items. It could even hold the bundles of greasy banknotes that merchants seem to favor. We plan to revisit this exciting topic in future issues."

Although I had somewhat expected this kind of sensationalism, the wild inaccuracies of the article left me stunned. Unable to share my frustration with anyone, I glanced across the desk at Prohor Savvitch, who had been watching me quietly. He held a copy of the Voice in his hand, apparently ready to pass it to me. Without a word, he took the News-sheet from me and handed over the Voice. He drew his nail along the margin of an article, marking the section he wanted me to read.

Prohor Savvitch was a peculiar man. A quiet bachelor, he rarely spoke to anyone in the office and wasn't close to any of us. He always had his own opinions but disliked sharing them. He lived alone, and almost none of us had ever visited his home.

This is what I read in the Voice.

Everyone knows that we pride ourselves on being progressive and humanitarian, striving to keep up with Europe. But despite all our efforts and the work of our newspaper, we are still far from achieving true maturity. This was made clear by the shocking incident that took place yesterday in the Arcade—something we had long predicted.

A foreigner arrived in the capital with a crocodile, which he began exhibiting in the Arcade. We immediately welcomed this as a new and useful business for our great and varied country. But yesterday at four o'clock in the afternoon, an unusually stout man, apparently intoxicated, entered the shop, paid the admission fee, and, without any warning, jumped straight into the crocodile's jaws. Naturally, the crocodile was forced to swallow him, likely out of self-preservation, to avoid being crushed. Once inside the crocodile, the man reportedly fell asleep. Neither the shouts of the foreign proprietor, the terrified cries of his family, nor even threats to call the police had any effect. From inside the crocodile came only laughter and a promise to "flay him," though the poor creature, struggling to digest such a massive meal, shed tears in vain.

As the saying goes, "An uninvited guest is worse than a Tartar." But this unwanted visitor refused to leave. How can we explain such barbaric behavior? It only proves our lack of culture and brings shame upon us in the eyes of foreigners. This reckless display of Russian temperament has found yet another bizarre outlet.

What could the man's motive have been? Was he seeking a warm and cozy home? There are plenty of good, affordable lodgings in the city, many equipped with gas-lit staircases, running water, and hall-porters. Why choose a crocodile?

We also want to draw attention to the cruel treatment of animals. It must be extremely difficult for the crocodile to digest such a large meal all at once. Now the poor creature lies swollen to the size of a mountain, suffering unbearable agony and awaiting death. In Europe, laws have long been in place to punish inhumane treatment of animals. Despite our European-style pavements and architecture, we are still far from shedding our outdated habits.

As the saying goes, "Though the houses are new, the traditions are old." And the houses aren't always new—at least not their staircases. We've often reported in our paper about the decayed wooden staircase in the home of the merchant Lukyanov in the Petersburg Side. This staircase has long posed a danger to Afimya Skapidarov, a soldier's wife who works there and frequently carries water or firewood up the steps.

Finally, as we predicted, the inevitable happened: yesterday evening, she fell while carrying a basin of soup, breaking her leg. Whether Lukyanov will now repair the staircase is uncertain; Russians often act only after disaster strikes. In the meantime, Afimya has been taken to the hospital.

Similarly, we've argued that porters in the Viborgsky Side, who clear mud from the wooden streets, should pile it neatly rather than splashing it onto pedestrians' legs. That's how it's done in Europe. And so on, and so on.

"What is this?" I asked in confusion, looking at Prohor Savvitch. "What does it all mean?"

"What do you mean?" he replied.

"Why, they pity the crocodile instead of Ivan Matveitch!"

"So what? Even an animal deserves pity—a mammal, after all. We have to keep up with Europe, don't we? They care deeply about crocodiles over there, too. He-he-he!"

With that, the peculiar old Prohor Savvitch buried himself in his papers and refused to say another word. I stuffed the Voice and the News-sheet into my pocket, along with as many old newspapers as I could find, intending to bring them to Ivan Matveitch for his evening entertainment. Though it was still hours until evening, I left work early and headed to the Arcade to observe from a distance and listen to people's opinions. I expected a large crowd and turned up the collar of my coat to brace for it. Feeling slightly self-conscious— publicity is unfamiliar to us—I resolved to put aside my personal discomfort in light of the extraordinary nature of this incident.

Thank you for Reading

You've Just Read a Piece of the Greatest Library Ever Rebuilt

Thank you for reading.

This book is one of thousands we're restoring, reimagining, and translating as part of the **Modern Library of Alexandria** — a global movement to preserve and share humanity's most important ideas.

What was once lost to fire and time is now rising again — not just as memory, but as living, breathing knowledge, freely accessible to all.

What You Can Do Next:

- **Keep Reading.**

  Discover more legendary works — in beautiful print, audiobook, or digital form — at LibraryofAlexandria.com.

- **Build Your Own Library.**

  Every title is available as a paperback, hardcover, or collectible boxset — at true printing cost. Craft a personal library worthy of display.

- **Spread the Light.**

  Share this book. Tell others about the movement. Help us translate every timeless work into every language, so no reader is ever left behind.

By finishing this book, you've already taken part in something extraordinary.

Join us at LibraryofAlexandria.com

Together, we're rebuilding the greatest library the world has ever known.

With appreciation,
The Modern Library of Alexandria Team

Visit:

www.libraryofalexandria.com

Or scan the code below: